50p

D0518801

Dear Pup

Letters to a Young Dog

Dear Pup

Letters To a Young Dog

Diana Pullein-Thompson
Illustrated by William Rushton

BARRIE & JENKINS

LONDON

First published in Great Britain in 1988 by
Barrie & Jenkins Ltd
289 Westbourne Grove, London W11 2QA

British Library Cataloguing in Publication Data
Pullein-Thompson, Diana
  Dear pup.
  1. Pets: Dogs – Humour
  I. Title
  636.7'00207

ISBN 0 7126 2136 9

Designed by Carol McCleeve
Printed by Printer Portuguesa, Portugal

To Angus

With happy memories

Dear Pup,

If you had a taste for heroics, a loud voice, threatening stance and strong well-muscled body, I would say, "yes, be a guard dog." But you're not like that, are you, not deep down? It's a puppy fantasy. You're like me, clever, insecure, affectionate, demanding and possessive. You want to own someone and to have a nice house and garden. You want gourmet meals, lots of friends and tea out of porcelain saucers when you feel like it, and holidays in wild and wonderful places like Mull.

So, speaking from a wealth of experience, I advise you to choose a family with growing children and a comfortable car. Avoid theatrical people — they can't bear competition and we dogs always steal the show. Don't get carried away by Daimlers or Rolls Royces. The rich are telephone-mad and talk endlessly about exchange rates and take-overs while you're aching for your dinner. They selfishly bar dogs from their swimming pools, even in the hottest weather. They will, without a backward glance, take off in jumbo jets for foreign places leaving you bereft by an empty barbecue set.

If you think a family might be too much of a pawful, look out for a jolly middle-aged woman in sensible shoes — avoid the melancholy kind. The chances are that such a lady will become totally devoted to you, so long as you tread carefully, paw by paw, and insinuate yourself into every aspect of her life. Aim to become INSEPARABLE, only curb your affectionate

W R O N G .

nature when she misbehaves or you need peace and quiet.

Middle-aged men are less predictable. Some make excellent companions, others care too much about their work. A few want to be macho, and may use you to show off their capacity for domination. Remember that in many houses the woman still rules supreme in the most important room, the kitchen. But not ALL. A domestically-minded man can be a dog's best friend.

Dear Pup, I must leave the decision in the end to you. Bruin, Bimbo and Tato have arrived in a red car, and we're off to Richmond Park.

Love and licks,

Suki

RIGHT.

Dear Pup,

Oh, bones and biscuits, I hope you've done the right thing, by choosing a young married couple. People in love are too tied up with each other to pay proper attention to a new and inexperienced puppy.

So they left you to sleep on a cold floor in the kitchen! And you cried all night for your warm bed and brothers and sisters. And when they came down your people threw up their hands in horror at the puddles. And in your agitation you chewed up three tea towels, a pair of slippers, a purple oven glove, a cheque book and a five pound note. Pup, that was a dreadful thing to do. I was turned out in the street for less. You must control yourself. Those things are BELONGINGS and dogs are meant to guard, not eat, BELONGINGS.

So they cleaned up, took you for a walk on the lead and went off to work. Didn't they feed you at all? And then you howled; is that right? You pointed your nose at the kitchen ceiling and, sitting on your haunches like a love-lorn wolf, you gave one of those long, long cries that turns human blood cold. And there was a COMPLAINT. A letter through the door which you would have eaten had you not been locked in the kitchen. And you made another pool and, in your agitation, ate a cushion.

Oh, Pup, how can I advise you? You've landed yourself with a couple of ignorant half-wits who do not understand the functions of the canine body. The only hope is that a neighbour may take pity on you. Otherwise you must RUN AWAY and find yourself a new home, and that's a big and dangerous decision to take.

Keep in touch. Keep wagging. Try to show your people how much you need them and take every opportunity to demonstrate that you expect to share their life in every way.

And keep up the howling.

My person is waiting with my lead in her hand. There are turkey breasts in the refrigerator, so I must keep on the right side of her.

Clearly your humans need training and you're too young to take on the job. I'll write again on my return when the fresh air may have set my brain buzzing.

A thousand friendly sniffs,

Suki

Dear Pup,

Yes, humans with a mania for cleanliness are such BORES and miss so much in life. And what is an intelligent dog to think when her people buy mud packs for their faces and then have hysterics if she brings the stuff in FREE on her paws? It's all so maddeningly inconsistent!

I try to put myself in my people's shoes. Supposing their house is to them like my basket is to me? I don't want other dogs' dirt mixed up with my pillow and rugs. And if any of my friends left a dead rat or bird there, I would bark my head off. So be patient, try to understand and give your people a little longer to settle down with you.

Lots of love, dear Pup, from your old friend, Suki

Dear Pup,

You are about to be TURNED OUT. I feel this in my bones, because I know how people like yours behave. So here's my advice:

Stay in one area to learn ins and outs. Remember self-pity is a down-grader. You're a tough little love-child with no in-breeding to weaken you.

Scrounging and scavenging can be both a challenge and an adventure. (Even a humble baked beans tin is a trophy among the down-and-outs, so long as there's juice in the bottom.) I promise you, bones do abound in the most unpromising places, since human teeth are too blunt to eat them. You'll find soft-hearted ladies in parks feeding birds. Bare your teeth and the proudest pigeon and jauntiest magpie will take flight. Hang around fish and chip shops at midday and in the evenings. Don't despair if no one offers you a morsel; you will find chunks of the nation's favourite dinner adhering to paper thrown in the bins outside. All foreign takeaway shops offer possibilities for persuasive, discerning dogs – happy indeed is the stray who finds a half-eaten carton of food. Kebabs, if you come across them, provide a never-to-be-forgotten experience.

Bed-times are sad times, but don't risk the open shed; someone may shut the door and, without knowing it, leave you to starve. A sheltered nest in the bushes is probably safest, although many dogs, like stray cats, swear by doorsteps.

When tired of the great outside, make for the nearest pet shop. Enter boldly with a customer. The owners HAVE to be animal lovers and can't turn you down in front of a patron. At worst you'll be given a dry biscuit and bowl of water. At best a plate of meat. If not offered accommodation, follow some sweet-faced lady home, slip into her place and settle down at once, as though you have been adopted. Assume she WANTS you. Sweet-faced ladies hate to DISAPPOINT or to be thought CRUEL, even by the humblest puppy. If this fails, you will find yourself at the POLICE STATION, which isn't as bad as it sounds. You're a blameless orphan, NOT a criminal. Many policemen are as soft as toffee when it comes to animals. Your immediate aim now is to avoid being banished to kennels in the backyard. Make yourself small, shiver like pampas in a strong breeze, snuggle up to anyone who is not answering the telephone, checking the computer, interviewing criminals or victims or dashing to a police car. Policewomen's laps are cosy if you can reach one. Lick hands whenever opportune, but don't yap or bark. If all humans are busy, curl up into a tight ball out of the way and feign sleep. No decent person likes to disturb an exhausted dog.

If you do land up behind bars looking at the sort of biscuits you hate most, keep CHEERFUL. It's not your fault that there was no one WORTHWHILE on duty. Some policemen and women are too THICK to recognise a canine jewel when they see one. Use this melancholy time to take stock of yourself before the hurly-burly of the dog home. Decide how you can do better next time.

Love and licks,

Suki

16

Dear Pup,

So my prediction was right, and here you are in a
Home for Lost and Abandoned Dogs. Well, I came
out of that experience with all plumes flying and
I'm sure you can too, so keep your chin up.

Like you I suffered from the class-system and, while
the pedigree dogs basked in individual kennels, I
was pushed into a crowded run for young bitches
without papers, *hoi-polloi*. But console yourself
with the thought that true dog lovers know that
crossbreds – the word "mongrel", as out-dated as
"nigger", will never cross my lips – have the highest
IQs and the strongest constitutions. Proud pekes,
prancing poodles and graceful wolfhounds will be
snapped up by those who want to make an
impression. Men will make a bee-line for alsatians,
labradors, retrievers and Dulux sheepdogs.
Shopkeepers will want the Rottweilers. Gentle
philanthropic ladies the forsaken greyhounds;
dressy females the Shih-tzus. But, Pup, don't let
your heart sink into your pads; someone will see
the beauty shining in your eyes and that air of
joyful optimism which makes you so enchanting.
Whatever happens, keep your tail up. Nobody wants
a dreary dog. You will learn to bare your teeth and
fight for your share at the feeding trough, but when
visitors come, wear your sweetest expression.
Women are for you, I think, best, but turn away
from timid elderly ladies who may want your

company so much that they will never let you off the lead. Leave them to the pomeranians and Tibetan spaniels, who can fit into a shopping bag. Remember, no one will choose you the first week, because there are seven days in which your hateful owners may claim you. But don't waste this important time. REHEARSE, REHEARSE, REHEARSE. Charm everyone who looks through the wire mesh, whether or not you fancy them. Your future depends on your expertise. But luck always plays a part.

I chose a middle-aged woman and only discovered afterwards that she already belonged to a delightful collie, Angus, who became my mentor; she had a large garden, two children and a husband who, after a few inevitable teething troubles, became a dear and close friend and the best provider of meal-time juicies.

Oh dear, Pup, I think of you often as I lie in my padded floral bed or take my person out for a jaunt in the park or ride in my Vauxhall Cavalier. But if you're anything like your mother, whom I knew so well from my Birmingham days, you'll come through wagging.

Licks and love, Suki

Dear Pup,

Well done! My congratulations! It sounds as though
you have chosen well this time. But why Mopsy?
What a name for a dog! Can you fit the picture it
conjures up? Are you soft and funny enough? Of
course you do have that extraordinary tuft of hair
on top of your head, but I remember your mother
had a hard core and a touch of dignity. You may be
cute and cuddly now, but when you're fully grown
you're going to be like a real dog, not a mop. If I
were you, I would show the tougher side of my
nature.

Suki has a certain hardness in it which I like. You
know, my people used to tell their more class-
conscious friends that I was a Tasselled Afghan
Hunting Dog, because of my courage in the deepest
undergrowth and my speed in open fields, and the
friends never knew whether to take them seriously.
And I was tremendously pleased and Angus looked
down his long nose and beamed his approval.
Angus, you see, was a real aristocrat, related to the
famous Pattingham Pacemaker and as neurotic as a
battery hen, but he taught me manners. Oh yes!

"Suki," he would say. "You're not in a Dogs' Home
now. Pause before you eat, then chew slowly,
savouring every mouthful. Afterwards find your
person and say 'thank you'. This shows breeding and
ensures that your next meal will be at least as edible."

You haven't told me whether your people are fat or thin, tall or short or, more important, strong smelling. Do they dowse themselves in toilet waters and scents or are they NATURAL. I like natural people best. They have a certain honesty about them.

Well, this little note is only to wish you luck. And now I'm off to accompany my friend, Tato, to the vet. Being a pekinese, Tato sees himself as some sort of Chinese emperor, but inside he's as shaky as a moth in a net. And he has INTERNAL problems. If he were not so afraid of losing face, he would be out of that place before they could switch on the computer. But he's a brave little button and I'm fond of him!

A lick on your nose and three for each ear,

Suki

Dear Pup,

The GARDEN is your very own territory. Patrol it regularly and if you feel bullish, mark it out as your male friends do, avoiding vegetables, if any. Chase out trespassing cats. Bury bones in shady corners away from flowers, and try to remember that lawns

are for sunbathing and games, not EXCAVATION. If you have the patience to lie on them like a stone lion, very still and gazing into the distance, your people will suspect blue blood, even if you haven't a single Cruftian forebear.

Excuse a meagre note. I'm about to be dragged off for a dental examination. Ooch what a poor pooch I am!

Licks, Suki

Dear Pup,

You are suffering from an identity problem. The choice of your name is the key to how your people want to see you: a little mad in a most endearing way, a skip-and-a-jump dog with a waggly tail, who hasn't quite grown up, very affectionate but easily disappointed. Play on this, Mopsy, develop a HURT look in your eyes which will melt the hardest human heart. Now, if they had called you Skipper or Sheba they would have misjudged you and expected a more commanding presence. Once you have accepted that you don't want to be a guard, a loner, a wild dog, or a stray, you must try to learn the gentle art of managing humans and recognise that you are a small and delightful half-grown dog, who will win her way by PERSUASION and CHARM and the theatrical streak which has come with your poodle blood.

At the moment I think you are barking too much and acting too little. Looks and gestures are often more appealing. A raised paw, a touch, a lick, a sigh or a significant shake or, as you get bolder, a warm doggie embrace, say more than a thousand barks. Above all cultivate the STARE, for who can resist dark eyes focussed like a torch's beam on their face? A long look mesmerises, enchants or arouses those innate guilty feelings which make humans so malleable. It frequently turns anger into benevolence and meanness into generosity. And,

Mopsy, there are several kinds of stare. The ASTONISHED, which is popular among Old Cruftians, suggests that your people have forgotten their manners and forsaken their promises, so lowering

them in your estimation to depths you never believed possible. The EAGER shames those who are about to let you down. The REPROACHFUL will bring that deserved second helping out of the refrigerator. And the PATHETIC — much favoured by cocker spaniels — persuades humans to forget their bills and switch on that electric fire or welcome you, after all, into the best room with the comfiest sofa. Eyeball to eyeball, never allow your gaze to stray from the face of your person until the concession you want has been granted. He who stares longest wins. That is a cardinal fact.

I scent criticism in your last letter. Dear Pup, I am not complacent about my own success, which has taken me ten years of untiring effort to achieve. Only now am I reaping the full benefit of my hard-earned expertise. And, far from boasting, I wish only to pass on to you the seeds of my own experience so that you may be spared the mistakes I made. We dogs must hang together in this human-dominated world and I want to share with you my happiness.

Suki

Dear Pup,

Sorry to lecture you. But the first weeks in a new home are absolutely CRUCIAL. If there is another dog, learn from its behaviour. Otherwise concentrate on obliging in EVERY way until you are ESTABLISHED. Don't howl if you're expected to sleep under the stairs or in the scullery. You will wheedle your way out in time. If your itchy teeth are uncontrollable and you have not been given anything delectable to chew from the pet shop, pick on old and little used things, like the worn head of a broom or faded and tattered dish-cloths. Eat meals gratefully, be clean and affectionate. Listen carefully and you will learn the humans' language far faster than they will learn yours. Concentrate on words vital to your happiness: DINNER, WALK, CAR, SHOPPING, and so on.

Life won't be easy, but if you start off on the right paw it will get better and better as you train your people to give you all the love and appreciation you undoubtedly deserve.

In great haste: we're going out to tea with an author down the road and I'm dying to have another look round her house — one of my hobbies!

Anyway, keep wagging. Loads of licks,

Suki

Dear Pup,

Clearly your people are dying to show you off and long for gratitude. So if they arrange lovely walks, why not go over the top a bit with your praise, smiling up into their faces, prancing playfully and licking their hands? Mix charmingly with other dogs, keep away from roads and come to heel when told. If taken to the country, make it a heyday. Swim in rivers, lakes and ponds. Inspect all rabbit warrens, enjoy hedgerows, give sheep and deer a wide berth even if they ask to be chased, and keep away from bulls and bullocks — some dream of turning dogs into plum jam. Your humans will think your excellent behaviour reflects their sound judgement, expert training and unerring good taste. When their friends say, "Oh how clever the Ricketts were to find that dear, good, little dog," you have the base on which to build an entirely satisfying partnership.

Good luck. Love and licks, Suki

Dear Pup,

I'm sorry I forgot to say, "Don't shake yourself near humans after swimming." A ruined white frock is a serious matter to some people. But I don't think they should have SLAPPED you. After all, you are only three months old and they were looking hot, and any normal person would, in the circumstances, be

glad of a sprinkling of protein-rich green pond water. But don't worry, they'll get over it!

We all make mistakes. I had a good deal of trouble over HOLES at one time, but eventually there was an understanding, with no love lost. So cheer up.

Thinking of holes, it IS hard to know where to bury bones if you're kept indoors. I usually hide mine under my people's pillows — no visiting dogs are likely to look there — or on the sofa, under at least FOUR cushions so that no smell can possible escape.

Occasionally I get up to re-hide them in the early hours when worries loom large in a sensitive dog's mind.

Most bones must mature under earth, so DO get yours outside as soon as you can.

I hope this advice is useful. Don't be downhearted. Things are usually ironed out in the end.

A lick on the nose and two for each eye from your ever-loving Suki

P.S. Sometimes it is wise to move bones from under pillows BEFORE bedtime.

Dear Pup,

I do find HUNTING a vexed question. I confess that in my wilder moments I have been tempted to run with beagles, but I hunt for fun and never KILL. If you and your people find Bloodsports useful therapy, then please do the job quickly with one skilful bite. We must never sink to the level of cats. If your humans are around, lay the corpse at their feet with a modest wag. Otherwise it is entirely acceptable to devour the body, fur and all, if your stomach will stand it.

On that unpleasant note I shall close this letter and enjoy a little pre-dinner sunbathing on the lawn my people have laid for me.

Lots of licks, Suki

Dear Mopsy,

I am so delighted that you have found a circle of friends. Dogs who don't mix become so peculiar. As for your discussion on BEDS, I think it best to

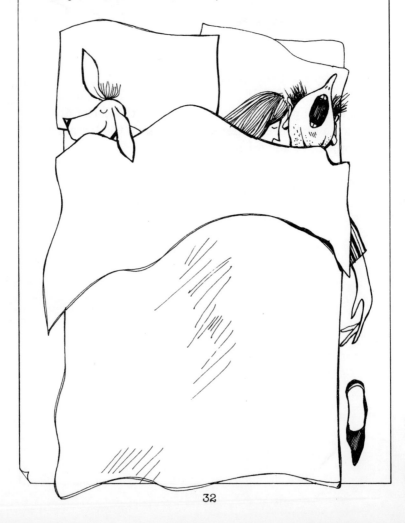

assume from the first that the BEST people share everything desirable with their dogs.

Once you are ESTABLISHED, it's a good thing to start each day with the words "I am EQUAL." But are you? Do you enjoy your share of that most luxurious and treasured possession? This is a vital question for us ALL. If your claim has been overlooked and you wake up on the floor, go to the bed itself, stand on hind legs and place paws close to human's face and try a tentative lick. If not welcomed, switch on PATHETIC stare (pedigree dogs may prefer the ASTONISHED). If this fails, plump for the bottom, avoiding feet, and edge up on stomach. A persuasive dog will soon have a corner of the pillow for its head and, in winter, will be valued INSIDE as a hot water bottle which does not lose heat during the night. But dogs larger than springer spaniels should not feel too downcast by rejection. It's a question of SIZE, not spiky claws or bad breath. Why not become a REPROACHFUL figure on the sofa instead?

Happy sleeping, love Suki

Dear Pupsy,

Of course you're right to be annoyed and upset. VACUUM CLEANERS are an ABOMINATION, and all drastic housework is unnecessary. Try snapping and barking at the bag and tube. If this doesn't stop operations, retire abruptly to a distant room and SULK until at least five minutes after the machine has been switched off and put away. Or, better still, go out into the garden and refuse to return for as long as you can bear your own company. If it's raining so much the better – a drenched puppy is a heart-rending reproach.

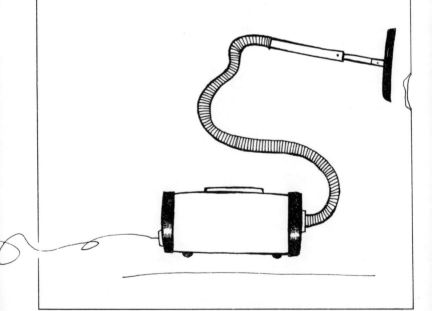

Of course it's barbaric to replace homely, doggy smells, which say this is Mopsy's place, with the cloying odours of air fresheners and furniture polish.

And, by the way, I lick stains on cushions and carpets to demonstrate that there is a quieter, safer way of cleaning. But I have to say that in the end I only manage to curtail or postpone operations. I hope you'll be luckier. Keep trying. I'm thinking of you.

Love and licks, Suki

Oh dear Mopsy,

I do agree. Compromises have to be made. Occasionally you may have to ADAPT, at least for a time, to deeply entrenched human faults and circumstances beyond your control.

A lively but imprisoned little dog I know was forced to turn her living-room into a wild and savage place. The settees are now mountains, the table a plateau and the stairs a terrifying cliff. When she leaps with fevered yaps from table to chair she is clearing a chasm, of mind-bending depths, with the courage of a stag. When she tears at the furnishings she is uprooting heather in her search for a rat of terrifying size and ferocity. (She has terrier blood.) Her person, one of those possessive elderly ladies I mentioned to you, loves this strange little dog so much that she allows the destruction but never lets her off the lead outside for fear she might run away. This is called EFFECT and CAUSE.

Anyway, Pup, never be afraid of slipping into fantasy. It's a wonderful outlet when the house is empty. You are alone and can't find your ball or bone. The night closes in and sleep won't come. On that sad note, I'll say goodbye for now, as my special person has arrived back from shopping with a nice little pack of raw mince in her bag. So I may be lucky.

Don't worry, you'll win in the end.

P.S. Later.

Only a MORSEL spared for me, but I'm off now to visit Fergus, who's waiting on the stairs for me — tea, leftovers and a sizeable lawn. Woofs!

Suki

Dear Pup,

You must become INDISPENSABLE. All humans, even
the most evil, crave love. Some are impossible, as we
know. But this time you have been adopted to fill an
emotional gap. (Husband unable to express feelings,
etc., etc.) So be affectionate and openly loving,
except when you are justifiably angry (vacuum
cleaners, no Christmas presents, and so on).

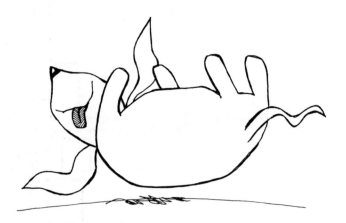

Just remember, we dogs are nicer to humans than
are their own species. We don't care what colour
they are, whether they are fat or thin, young or old,
so long as they can walk. We don't turn a hair at

acne, bunions, a huge nose or bald head. We don't object if they pick their noses, leave false teeth on the sideboard or nail filings on the carpet. Once they are ours we do our best to cherish them, even if they say the same thing over and over again. We are, in fact, Mopsy, the finest social workers in the world. And we cost the State NOTHING. Once you are indispensable, begin to demand your rights, with charm and firmness.

Much love,

Suki

Dear Pup,

Ball games can be a healthy pastime for humans, if you like that sort of thing.

Choose male rather than female partners, they're better throwers. Place ball in front of right foot, step back two paces and bark sharply. Problems may arise over who is finally responsible for the ball when you've had enough. Train your humans to look for lost ones. After all, you've been doing all the running and it's not your fault you were bewitched by a blue-eyed husky.

My advice is limited because I don't retrieve myself and ball addicts bore me rigid.

We're just off to the Cotswolds, the passage is full of suitcases, so I must dash, but two licks and a big, big sniff from your ever-loving

Suki

Dear Mopsy,

No, I had a lousy weekend because the bird scarers kept me indoors. Now I'm old they give me the shivers. My people say no bullets are fired, but I think it's best to be on the safe side. An awful lot of pheasants get killed every year. And Angus knew a cat once who was shot by a professor practising with an air gun.

AnGus.

You ask how to behave on a car journey. But you don't say what kind of car your people have. If it's an estate, or even a hatch-back, you may be in trouble. It's best to assume from the first that you will occupy the passenger seat beside the driver, but don't complain too much if you're relegated to the back. This is quite acceptable and entails no loss of status. The position to avoid at ALL COSTS is the very rear amongst the suitcases, fodder or what-have-you. The situation is smelly, insulting and sick-making. If put there, immediately leap on to the back seat and snuggle up against the softest-hearted passenger; cherish her (or him) with a lick on the ear, a diffident paw on the knee and a charming head on a shoulder. This should do the trick.

If your humans are cruel and insensitive enough to fix bars to keep you in the luggage area, remain standing throughout the journey so blocking the driver's rear view; an action which ensures a seat with the passengers next time.

Happy driving.

Love Suki

Dear Puppy,

Sorry about the tummy rumbles. Don't ask for drastic changes in the timetable. Aim to advance your meals by about five minutes a day, until you have reached the best hour for yourself. Heavy hints may be necessary. If your mouth is the right shape (pekes' and pugs' are not, but I think yours is), fetch your bowl and place it at your special human's feet, then turn on EAGER stare. If this fails, enter kitchen, tail high, and sniff air appreciatively, pointing nose in the direction of hob or refrigerator, depending where food is. If nothing happens, switch to ASTONISHED and then PATHETIC stares. Finally BARK.

I know in my bones that you're going to succeed, but I am sorry to hear about your special person's selfishness over the chocolates. If she's putting on weight, there's a chance her doctor might prescribe more walking which could be good news for you. So keep wagging and think of her GOOD points. No human is perfect.

Luckily I only want chocolates on Christmas Day when they're very plentiful and most people feel UNselfish. Anyway, you'll be healthier WITHOUT them.

Licks from your ever-loving Suki

Dear Pup,

There's nothing sissy about you. All normal dogs with light or short coats should have a FIRE, but, sadly, few humans realise that we need warmth more than they do. Indeed, you may have to use all your powers of persuasion, delectable *sang-froid* and obstinate sitting-it-out tactics to win your RIGHTFUL place on the hearth. In my second home

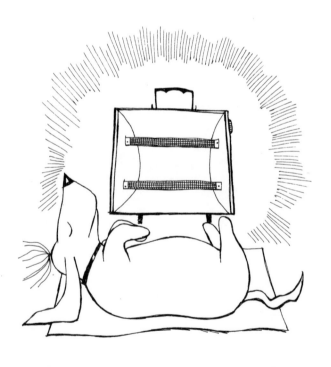

(see flyleaf) I was quick to assume that the smaller electric fires were turned on for ME and ME ALONE.

This is not as difficult as it sounds, for there is time, as your humans lean down to press on the switch, for you to take your place huddled very close to the bar itself, BEFORE the heat comes through. Your main justification for HOGGING is that humans can put on more clothes, whereas you have to make do with the same outfit ALL the year round. Mopsy, this is a battle you MUST win for your own comfort and well-being. After all the humans DO still feel warmth if they sit BEHIND you.

If you meet with extreme selfishness, you must resort at once to jungle laws by scratching trouser legs or nylon tights, with sharp claws. A wrongful set pattern (Humans Hog Fires) would be harmful to you and could even become ENDEMIC in the area, so upsetting for many miles around the correct social balance between man and dog, which has been established only after years of dedicated canine research, suffering and effort. Sorry to sound pompous, but this is a MOST serious matter. And remember you've been invited to live with these people so it would be utterly DISGRACEFUL to let you freeze.

Be FIRM. I look forward to hearing what happens.

Ever in my thoughts, Suki

Dear Pup,

BRUTE nearly always suggests anger and perhaps imminent attack, so do scarper if possible and hide in a dark, safe place.

BEAST is frequently only an expression of irritation, so snuggle-up and offer paw. If said with a grin, smile back and wag tail, because it could be part of a FOND joke.

If either of these words is *prefaced* with "handsome", "fine" or the like, they are compliments, which deserve a small bow and diffident wag.

DIRTY DEVIL denotes a doggy MISTAKE and possibly punishment, so a cooling-off period is essential. Disappear into the garden and avoid all human contact for at least half an hour.

MONKEY, LITTLE HORROR, SCROUNGER are affectionate rebukes, so roll over on to your back and offer your tummy for a rub – a form of apology which doubles up as soothing therapy for upset humans.

SWEETIE, DARLING, DEAR, TREASURE and other endearments should be met with tail-wagging and licks. It is wrong to behave like a peke and take them for granted, however grand you feel.

But do bear in mind, Mopsy, that everything can be altered by a change of tone, for humans have a very strange sense of humour and occasionally say the opposite to what they mean and then roar with laughter. "Sweetie" can be used with terrible irony when you rush into the clean kitchen with wet paws, or "Brute" with a rueful smile when you suddenly leap from a corner like a bullet from a gun.

My people are such talkers that at ten I am still learning!

Keep listening.

Love Suki

Dear Pup,

I am sorry your tummy rumbling still troubles you. I expect this little slice of cold weather has spiced up your appetite. Yes, I do share my people's meals as well as eating my own. At supper I concentrate on the man in the house because, being away during the day, he doesn't know how much I've eaten already. But don't count on steak and chicken every night and remember humans have an extraordinary habit of wrecking good meat with sauces and pepper when it would be better left holed-up in the garden for a few days.

If you're a choosy eater, make sure there's something worthwhile on the table before pulling out all the stops — HEAD ON KNEE, PLEADING PAW,

BESEECHING EYES etc., etc., — it's awful to be offered something disgusting, like lemon soufflé, after expending so much energy. And whatever happens, don't DROOL. Nobody wants volumes of spit on their clothes. Great Danes and Irish Wolfhounds may have the immense advantage of being able to rest their heads on the table, but our LITTLENESS appeals to the protective element present in the best humans' natures. Sometimes you may even be able to edge your way into laps at meal-times and point your nose.

I have a friend, quite a rough diamond actually, who is frequently given a seat at table by her rather eccentric but dog-besotted humans. She has taken the place of GRANDCHILD, a remarkable feat from which we can all learn something.

My own fear is that my people will become vegetarians or start that *nouvelle cuisine* lark which I hear, from a film producer's dog, has hit America.

It's raining cats and rats now, so I'm going to slip away to my biggest basket and dream of sunshine and of the snow that tingles me so deliciously.

A kiss and a sniff from your ever-faithful friend,

Suki

Dear Mopsy,

Over-petting is a dreadful problem. But since your poodle friend's human is adolescent, I think the phase will pass. Yet every dog has a right to some PEACE and QUIET. I suggest he should try to moderate rather than end petting. When he's had enough he should roll himself into a rigid ball — no one likes stroking or kissing a hard unyielding object — and turn his back. Or leave the room and settle under some low piece of furniture, a bed or coffee table, perhaps, where cuddling is not really possible.

When the time is right your friend should make his own approach, place paw on knee and let his eyes speak for him: "Now I'm in the mood, you may stroke me if you like!"

The heavy petters need us more than we need them, but usually, even among middle-aged people, the condition is only temporary. The best cure, outside your control, is the arrival of a new friend, generally of the opposite sex. The sufferer may then go to the other extreme and NEGLECT you. Oh dear, life is never easy, and humans can be a trial.

Love and licks, Suki

Dear Pup,

Of course I had faults, too, when young. My paws dug holes in the lawn if Angus refused to play with me, and when the man in my life came home he was angry. He carried me to the holes and shook me, saying "BAD, BAD," and I was terribly upset, but Angus, who liked to provoke humans now and then, was greatly amused.

One evening when our people were out Angus said:

"You're still puppy spirited, aren't you?"

And I said: "Yes, of course."

And he said: "I was so afraid you might be a prig. Prigs are such a bore. Do you want to join in some fun?"

Angus was charismatic, tri-coloured with superb black eye make-up, laced with gold. He was my mentor, so I said, "Yes".

"Good, we're going to teach THEM a lesson," he told me. "They've left us alone one evening too many. Come on, use your teeth."

In no time we had torn up one of our smaller people's furry slippers, three tea-towels and a dish cloth. Then we dug up a carpet and rolled a rug in front of the front door, so that it would be hard to open. We were about to destroy a few fluffy toys when our people returned and started to push their way in. Then Angus told me to follow him upstairs.

"But we must welcome them!" I cried.

"Don't be silly. They're going to be angry," he said.

We hid in the bathroom, but they got in and shouted at us, and remembering how I had lost my last home, I rolled over on my back and offered them my tummy.

But Angus snarled and then I knew I mustn't think of him as my mentor any more. He had made a MISTAKE and caused me to upset the person who had rescued me from the Dogs' Home, while I had been desperately trying to establish myself through my capacity to love and enchant.

Of course we were both quickly forgiven, although the occasion has never been forgotten and might well, as you know, have cost me my second home.

So you see I have been led astray, too.

In haste – I have a tea appointment –

Love and an earful of licks, Suki

Dear Mopsy,

I don't know how to take your news — a BABY on the way! In my experience, infants are dangerous, because they think our eyes are jelly and our tails bell-pulls. And they cry and cry and cry, and there's NOTHING you can do about it.

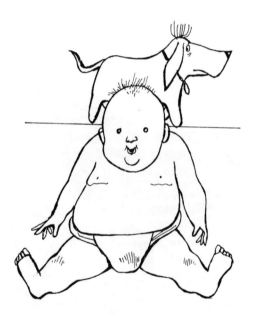

After giving birth, your person will turn against canine tongues, so don't wash her baby's face, however dirty it may be. Many mothers lose all sense of proportion and may forget dogs' meals. But, of course, you MUST become INVOLVED in looking after this new member of YOUR family. I think it would be wisest if you became a WATCHDOG. Bark whenever a stranger approaches pram or cot. On the other paw, if you have been bought mainly for your beauty, you merely have to walk decoratively beside the little darling, because, like it or not, you have now become part of a vignette. I don't know whether to congratulate or commiserate but I do wish you the best of luck!

A thousand licks, Suki

Dear Pup,

Do explain to your springer friend, Fetch, that his constant barking is the cause of his person's hysterical behaviour. He must STOP or she will go crazy and attack him with a broom or spade. I've actually seen that happen. Loud barking should be kept for emergencies. No one trusts a dog who cries "Vivisectionist!" too often. If he feels deprived of walks, he must get his way through charm and tact, not noise. Maybe he should try to attach himself to

a park keeper, who might offer to be a day-time minder. I've seen that happen, too. Tell him to use his brain and THINK. Dogs who deafen us all whenever they feel out of sorts are boors and an insult to canine intelligence.

By the way, I wouldn't have been so excited about the baby if I had known there are another three months to go, but I'm sorry about the incessant knitting. It's infuriating to be ignored. Why don't you make a great fuss of the man in your house?

Humans are just as jealous as we are.

Try it anyway.

Lots of friendly sniffs from your ever-loving

Suki

Dear Mopsy,

I am so sorry that I didn't brief you for Christmas, the most extraordinary day in the year, but I'm glad you were at least given one slice from the turkey's breast.

Of course being old now I recognise the signs weeks before and am always up early on the actual MORNING, eagerly awaiting my bag of presents. It's perfectly usual for some families to spend over an hour in church working up an appetite for later FEASTS. I don't think you would enjoy a service, but

you should be included in ALL other celebrations and, oh, how disgusted I am that no one bought you a present!

If this happens NEXT YEAR, show your dissatisfaction in the following ways:

    1) Examine everyone else's presents with the UTMOST interest and then search gift wrappings and bags with minute care as though expecting juicy morsels or toys for yourself.

    2) Switch on ASTONISHED and REPROACHFUL stares alternately.

    3) Follow special person round house, sniffing air, and turning on EAGER stare whenever drawer or cupboard is opened.

    4) If you have not received a present by lunch time, steal sweets or chocolates from table or tree, and then smile cheerfully, as though you believe these cheap offerings to be the presents no one remembered to give you.

5) Sit beside baby and jump up expectantly whenever it is handed a gift and, finally, if still neglected, gently intercept one for yourself whether you like it or not. This is called MAKING A POINT.

I do hope your humans will turn out well. I am sorry they seem a trifle thick, but steady training has its own REWARDS and, as time goes on, you may feel justifiable pride in their improvement.

Keep trying anyway.

Commiseration and licks, Suki

Dear Pup,

No, of course, you mustn't come between married couples in bed. It's best to lie against your special person's body, near the edge, so if there is any hanky-panky you don't get entangled with it, and can drop nonchalantly to the floor. If they seem very lovey-dovey, stay in your basket. But if a quarrel erupts BARK. It's very important to nip that sort of thing in the bud, and a dog can play an incalculable role in keeping couples together.

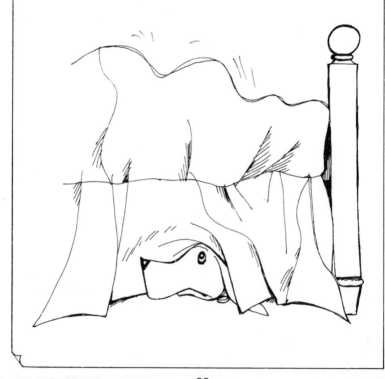

Angus was always adamant on this point and would actually nip the person he considered at fault . . . always the female which was, I think, wrong. But I suppose he felt it important to keep on good terms with the best ball thrower.

Love and licks, Suki

Dear Pup,

All right, all right, so I lied about my age and your mother says I was thirteen in the summer of 1987. Her memory is better than mine. But I FEEL and LOOK ten and that is what matters. I forget my years because my friends are younger than me and I enjoy life so much, running, swimming, rolling and chasing wildly on the Green. And I'm bored rigid by stuffy old dogs who winge on about their aches and pains. I ignore my rheumatism and spondylosis.

If you start counting time, Mopsy, life isn't fun any
more. Although I must say Tato did openly celebrate
his tenth birthday right here on the Green eighteen
months ago with food flown in from Athens and a
cake made specially in the shape of a bone with ten
candles. What a party that was! All the dogs
wearing ribbons. Sixty guests and only one canine
scrap. And do you know a policewoman popped over
to check the balloons, which was pretty nice of her
considering how many burglars there are on the
loose. Quite a day! But I withdrew quietly and held
court for my friends along the fence by the railway.

"Greta Garbo," someone called me, which I think
may have been a compliment, but I'm not sure. I
would have MIXED and CIRCULATED if there hadn't
been so many terriers yapping on and on about this

and that. I think even Tato found them distracting, try as he would to be the perfect emperor host.

Anyway, enough said. My people don't know my birthday date, so I've never had a celebration — a bit of a let-down, really. But one can't expect everything in life.

Write me a nice letter next time, Mopsy, and stop the undercover work — there's a good Pup.

Licks and love from your youthful old friend,

Suki

Dear Mopsy,

I'm sorry you're still having trouble over the fire. I chose a small one-bar affair, which runs very cheaply. Try hunching your back; there's a particular way of doing this which melts the hardest human heart. And don't forget to whimper and shiver. If all this fails, the REPROACHFUL stare might help.

But don't worry, when the baby's born things will get back to more or less normal.

Love Suki

Dear Pup,

Personal hygiene is tremendously important. Beard and cheeks stained by countless dinners are really rather awful for everyone else. So do make an effort. I wash my face twice daily, licking the inside of my wrists and forearms so that they can be used as damp sponges. (I learned this wheeze from a sleek cat called Pushkin.) They're good for removing eye peeps too. Angus used the carpets as table napkins after every meal, but my people didn't appreciate that habit very much. I think a clean, shining face is most attractive and not even your best dog

friends are likely to be interested in what your last six or even seven meals were.

I must close now, because we're off to visit an elderly relation in Luton. There are no doggy post offices or canine smells of any note in that town, but quite a dinky little garden and a grey-haired lady who thinks I'm the world's cleverest dog. So I'm hoping for a slice of roast beef.

Love and licks, Suki

Dear Pup,

I didn't realise you were thinking of mating with
Fetch yourself. Isn't he rather big and do you really
fancy a springer spaniel? I've known one for years,
called Kes. He's besotted with guns, which doesn't
leave much time for love-mating. He's very
attractive but personally I prefer the sort of dog
who stands on his own paws, like those latchkey
crossbreds who used to hurry over the pedestrian
crossing in Birmingham punctually at half past five
every evening when the fish and chip shop opened.
Now *they* had true masculine resilience. And really
knew their way around. Of course I'm very fond of
Tato, Bruin, Bimbo and Fergus but I wouldn't
choose them to father my puppies, because they're
too soft and dependent. Do you know what I mean?
But I must leave you to run your own very personal
life and one dog's love is another dog's hate, and it's
all a matter of FEELING and WANTING. Angus always
seemed more interested in the messages than in the
females THEMSELVES. And my labrador friend Dido, a
great flirt, who's moved to Aberdeen, had a marriage
arranged by her humans with one of her own breed
– a devastatingly handsome young black dog –
which was never actually consummated. What do
your people think? Do consider this matter very
carefully and control any sudden and over-riding
impulse. Let me know what happens. I'm quivering
with envy and apprehension.

By the way, you've grabbed the wrong end of the stick. I love my people very, very much and they love me. Nevertheless, it is essential that we dogs should MANAGE our humans while letting them think the sock is on the other paw and they are managing us. Thereby lies happiness.

Lots and lots of licks from your ever-loving

Suki

Dear Pup,

I can't understand why you were bored after only five minutes at the tea party. There is so much to see and examine in other people's houses. I always go to kitchens first because quite often they harbour cat or dog food left in little dishes on the floor which should be eaten up straight away. And then there are a friend's belongings to inspect: his basket perhaps or bean bag, which are always

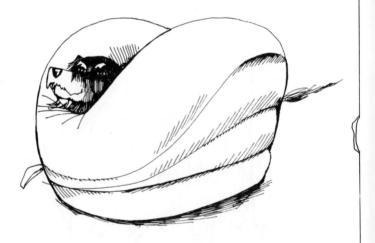

fascinating to try out, and maybe squeaky toys or balls. Afterwards I examine all the humans' things: knick-knacks are usually worth a quick sniff and if you can manage a *real* house inspection, you will soon know whether or not your friend has achieved a place on the bed, and, for some reason I don't understand myself, I always enjoy a quick look round the bathroom. Being a human-lover, I am, I suppose, deeply interested in how many loos, dresses, suits, walking sticks and such like people keep in their homes.

By five o'clock it's time to put on a show, just as the humans are running out of talk. Dash in, tail up, with one of your friend's toys, toss it in the air, and amaze them all with your juggling skills. If you have not been offered tea and biscuits, now is the time to make your disappointment clear.

Love and licks, Suki

Dear Pup,

Apropos — yes, I've picked up a spot of French from the man in our house, who likes to show off his accent now and then — of your recent letter about dog snobs, I lunched the other day with my special person's sister, Josephine, and a very nice lady who took a great liking to me.

"What breed is Suki?" she asked as she finished a plate of roast duck with trimmings.

"Tasselled Afghan Hunting Dog," my special person replied with her usual aplomb, never batting an eyelash.

"Oh, I say, how VERY interesting," the lady said. "I knew she was a PROPER dog by her head."

Can you imagine it, Mopsy? My head? Well, I suppose it has got a bit of spaniel about it. But had I been a bull terrier I would have given the game away with a crinkly smile. Being me, I kept a sober face and looked my admirer straight in the eye, so that she left thinking excitedly she had discovered an exotic new breed.

Well, Pup, that blows the top off this pedigree rubbish, doesn't it? You can share sniffs with your crossbred friends over THAT STORY.

Cousin Trixie, by the way, has "German Schnautzer, colour as to breed" written by her vet on her vaccination certificates. But she actually KNOWS who her father was and she is, she says, a mixture of alsatian, collie, cairn and, she thinks, poodle. But she has taken on the fierce character of a Schnautzer in keeping, she remarks rather grandly, "with current medical opinion".

So there you are AGAIN. These humans are not as clever as they think, and if only we knew more ourselves, we would recognise their mistakes. All the same, I do rather dote on mine, and they are sometimes so endearingly helpless that my heart melts in sympathy.

A lick for each ear and one for your nose, Suki

Dear Mopsy,

It's really too bad that you've been left with such an inconsiderate sister-in-law while your people enjoy foreign shores. She doesn't sound like a hostess to me. Of course, you're bound to MISS your hard-won rights to bed, armchairs and second helpings. And it's deeply disappointing to wait until lunch-time for your morning walk. But I don't think it was sensible to roll on that dead bird. Humans don't recognise a juicy smell when they meet it, and you knew in your heart that it would annoy. Revenge never pays off. Re-education is the only way. But is it worth wasting your skills on such a lump of stupidity for a stay of only a few more days?

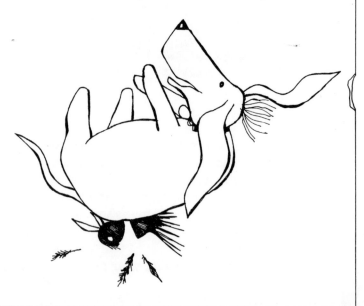

The important thing is to make it clear to your humans that you never want to return to such a miserable house. Give them a wild and wonderful welcome and rush from the horrible place without a backward glance. In future when this sister-in-law visits your home treat her like the vacuum cleaner.

Cheer up. It's nearly over. Licks and sympathetic wags,

$$Suki$$

P.S. Try to be happy. A happy dog makes a happy person and happy people are NICE and KIND and LOVING, three attributes you will sorely need after your difficult experience. Whenever your special human looks at you wag your tail; then she'll smile back and your moods will match. Matching good moods is a unique canine art. But remember, BAD moods are particularly infectious and can actually POISON atmosphere and make you ill. So eat, drink and be merry and don't reproach your people for leaving you. With luck you have another fifteen years to go.

Dear Pup,

Welcome home! Isn't this weather glorious? How I
bask in it. I've made myself two bowers, one for sun,
the other for shade. Well, London gardens are so
small that a dog must lay claim to certain areas at
the first sign of fine weather, otherwise there's no
space left.

I use my claws and teeth to clear my cool patch
amongst the shrubs. Well, it's always best to be a
little below lawn level for comfort. Now I've lost a
few teeth I find roots a bit of a problem, but I
manage to bite them through in the end. The sunny
spot is easy. I just plonk myself down and stretch
out on the south-facing side and my weight flattens
the earth, and that's that. No argument. My people
know it's MY garden too and, when you think about
FOOTAGE, I have far less than my share.

Mopsy, have you discovered BONE MEAL? Whenever
my special person plants something new she feeds
it with the stuff. Isn't that mad? I mean shrubs and
flowers don't have stomachs, do they? I wait until
she's back inside the house before I begin my
treasure hunt. Remembering my youthful problems
over HOLES, I don't dig. I just use my nose and a claw
now and then to sift the earth very carefully until I
taste the meal and then, ooch, it's so delicious!
Afterwards I try to nuzzle the earth back very
neatly, but I think my special person suspects

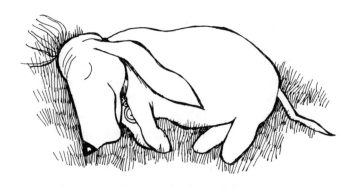

something because sometimes she offers me a handful of the meal which I always refuse with great dignity. It's much more exciting to find it for myself. And not even the TINIEST twinge of guilt troubles me, because it really is CRIMINAL to waste such a nourishing delight on plants. Maybe, it's all a game. Humans can be so devious sometimes.

Anyway, do ASSUME that you have special lying places and don't let your people cover every inch of the garden with useless pansies, marigolds, thorns and what-not. Many a dog has lost out on property matters through not making her wishes known soon enough. That prosperous old society the RSPCA has stated clearly that every dog needs a garden, so do go ahead with a crystal-clear conscience.

A thousand warm licks and lots of encouragement from a sun-soaked Suki

Dear Pup,

I try to be brave when I'm taken to the vet. I don't whine in the waiting room like other dogs, or wail like wretched cats. I talk to other patients to raise morale. It is only when I see my nice bearded, brown-eyed vet and the couch that my legs fail me.

Yet the other day when I had an upset stomach (not an operational job) I was quite glad to go. The vet stuck a needle into my back, just above the tail (ouch), and two hours later, I leapt off the bed at home, shook myself and suggested it was dinner-time. Amazing! Earlier I had been carried back from my morning walk. So vets, Pup, do have their USES.

In MY health centre the nurses are the ones to watch because they actually take dogs and cats AWAY for operations. When they enter the waiting room with a hospital collar in their hands, I leap on to my special person's knee and press myself like a leech against her chest. Sometimes they're after another patient, but if it's me they want, I find myself placed with many apologies into the nurse's arms and then – oooch – I know I'm in for one of those weird dream-ridden sleeps and an extraordinary caged awakening.

Anyway, I must tell you, Mopsy, my last dental operation changed my life. It was a pretty bad affair, a major tooth was deeply infected with an abscess and, after it was out, I felt a different dog. You've no idea! I stopped wanting my basket in the middle of the afteroon and retiring to bed at eight thirty p.m., and returned to my old habit of trying to get games started on the Green. That's a pretty hopeless ambition, by the way, because London dogs are not as high-spirited as those I knew in Birmingham. Some are too blasé. Others lack team spirit and are afraid of losing face or, quite simply, don't have stamina. Such a shame!

Listen, Mopsy, vets are expensive. Your people wouldn't take you unless they genuinely think you need a check-up.

Good luck. Keep your tail up. I shall be thinking of you. Love, Suki

Dear Pup,

I'm very sorry it didn't happen, but don't be too down-hearted. Puppies are, of course, darlings at first, but you might have been banished from the house, your armchair, your bed, everything, and probably kept outside on STRAW. (Is there a shed?) Or sent away to kennels. And your family might have been larger than you anticipated, eight or nine, perhaps, or even more. And since it was not an ARRANGED mating you might have been forced to leave home and hide the little darlings. I've seen a farm dog carrying her puppies from place to place, knowing they would be drowned if discovered. What a tragedy! The very thought makes me feel very small and miserable. And all the licking and cleaning! It's hard work, Mopsy. Oh yes, it's a terrible responsibility to bring unplanned puppies into the world.

And do remember, after a few weeks the little darlings have pin-sharp teeth but they'll suck and suck, fighting for the fullest teat without a single thought for you. And after a bit you will keep sneaking away for a bit of peace and quiet. You'll sit, a mournful figure on the doorstep, longing for your creature comforts. And you'll be glad to see them go.

Mopsy, I'm not suggesting you were WRONG to give your people the slip. I admire you for it. Why should we all miss out on love? But I'm urging you to be realistic and remember that motherhood is not all chicken, steak and bones.

So cheer up and do remember that you have your whole life still before you and a couple of quite reasonable humans to occupy your time and exercise your training skills. And perhaps you can have another try in six months time with a less cerebral, more experienced, dog.

P.S. I've just remembered — my friend Becky was turned out, when she was PREGNANT, that's how she finished up in Battersea Dogs' Home, along with all her darlings. Her story DOES actually have a HAPPY ending, but everything was pretty awful at the time.

My Friend
BECKY.

Dear Pup,

I know you were unlucky with that dreadful and unfeeling sister-in-law, but, even though the first night is always sad, it is POSSIBLE to enjoy a holiday WITHOUT your people. Some kennels even promote an exciting sense of CAMARADERIE (Bruin survives his in a wild poodle-pack whirl and returns home bursting with energy). But in a private home you must ADAPT and take a polite interest in ALL the ARRANGEMENTS. Humans like to SHARE plans, Mopsy. A mourning dog makes no friends.

Bruin.

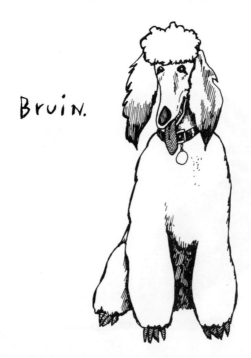

When left with my special person's elder sister, Josephine, I begin by shaking myself vigorously. (Shake out the old life, bring in the new.)

"Suki," I say. "Prick up your ears, wag your tail and put your best paw forward. And enjoy yourself." And by heavens I do, Mopsy. I do. I have a shark of a time. You'd be surprised. I twist Josephine round my littlest claw and eat so many chicken dinners I'm afraid I'll grow wings.

On the first morning I stretch very ostentatiously to show that I'm expecting ACTION and intend to join in EVERYTHING, especially the PEN Club, where authors congregate to listen to other authors, and walks in Battersea Park where I take a dip in the lake, not a REAL swim, but a one paw on the floor sort of thing.

Moments after breakfast I'm sitting on the passenger seat in Josephine's little old car watching London go by. Then I'm actually in her office – she runs PEN – where in winter I quickly take charge of a fire, listening to all the talk of prisoners and writing and all that, and welcoming guests. On my first visit Josephine felt I would be happier during FORMAL meetings outside in the car, but I soon put a stop to THAT – it's astonishing how hard I am to budge when I rebel – and now I have become a FAMILIAR FIGURE, even at Finance Meetings. Of course I'm absolutely NO trouble so long as we have a lunch break out of doors to keep Josephine in good shape, and, being an experienced dog of some intuition, I do know when SERIOUS matters are being discussed and quietness is essential. If I may drop you a morsel of advice, Mopsy, when off home territory develop a sense of OCCASION, learn when to slip into the background and become ornamental. There's something very pretty about a dog well arranged on a chair or bench, especially to eyes wearied by figures and sums. And NEVER rush in where sparrows fear to hop.

Pup, to be frank, I have sat at the feet of famous speakers (after helping out with any leftovers) and, feeling deeply and wonderfully appreciated, have returned home very full of myself, to be welcomed

on the Green by all my canine and human friends.
Troubled by guilt my special person is especially
sweet to me; chicken dishes appear as if by magic —
she's competing with her sister — and so merry is
my reception that, although I dearly love my home,
I am glad I went away.

I mustn't rattle on, but I am anxious that you
should not automatically sink into a Depression
when "Holiday" enters the conversation or
suitcases appear in the bedroom.

Love and licks from your ever-loving friend,

Suki

Dear Pup,

Yes, "thank you's" are incredibly important because of the intense human need to feel APPRECIATED.

Without unstinting doggy praise the more sensitive may actually slide into DEPRESSION, a serious condition which according to Angus is like staring eternally without hope into a deep dark pit.

I always show my gratitude with a lick. There was a time when I thought the lips were the right place for this, because human-watching soon taught me that very affectionate people kiss each other on the mouth. But no one seemed to like this as much as I had expected, so I have now decided to lick the hands of those I don't know very well and the noses of my special friends, such as Bruin's, Tato's and Fergus's people, and, of course, Josephine, because she's the best hostess I know. Angus mistakenly thought a nose push in the crotch was the right way of saying "Thanks, old bean!" but I soon perceived this was a cause of embarrassment. Kind chauffeurs should be rewarded with a lick on the neck which is easily given from the back seat of a car, and is always well received.

It's up to you to decide your particular form of thanks. But I must stress again that some expression of gratitude is essential if you are to become INDISPENSABLE.

A thousand licks, Suki

93

Dear Pup,

You must NOT be hoity-toity. Neighbours are very IMPORTANT and can be life-saving. My only regret at moving into this house, which is bigger, comfier and warmer than the last, is that Tato and his people no longer live next door. Mopsy, it is no exaggeration to say that I CAPTURED their hearts.

NeigHbourS.

Very soon a neat little opening was made so that Tato and I could use each other's gardens and exchange niceties whenever we wished.

But the most important aspect of this special arrangement was the LEFTOVERS. Tato, being a butterfly peke of minute and most fastidious appetite, doesn't eat like a real dog. He is fed by hand, morsel by morsel and, even so, makes a point of leaving part of his dinners and refusing to have the same menu twice running. So, to spare his humans the heartbreak of chucking the rejected delicacies into the dustbin, I used to pop round two or three times a day to offer my services.

Anna, his special person, and I came to a fairly rough and ready, but wholly satisfactory agreement about this and I remained polite even when disappointed. But when Anna's mother came from Greece, oh woofs, she was so impressed by my manners – my thank you's were impeccable and Angus, you will remember, taught me how to savour food appreciatively – that she fell into the habit of COOKING choice little dishes specially for me, wonderful, wonderful meals, Mopsy, laced with the most superb sauces.* And she could not bear to DISAPPOINT, so whenever I went round, even seven times a day, there was always a little SOMETHING waiting just for me.

*This letter carries a Government Health Warning – Editor

Well, sadly, with cats as neighbours here, that's all in the past, although I do drop in on Tato two or three times a week just to help out. But it does show what CAN be achieved if a dog approaches neighbourly duties with tact, dedication and, of course, CHARM. Cheese — I mean butter — up those people next door. Apart from leftovers, if anything goes wrong they can save the day. Angus — no, I'll tell you that another time. The thought of those sauces has ruined my concentration.

Keep charming. Love from a hungry Suki

P.S. *After dinner.* On second thoughts: if your neighbour is still a basset hound — bad luck! — there won't be even a sniff of a leftover. In fact he'll be after yours. Those pack dogs are the very devil. Bury your bones deep and hide spare biscuits. What a whacking shame!

More licks, Suki

Dear Pup,

Yes, I do believe that a young dog should entertain humans (especially babies) who, poor things, miss so much through being nasally handicapped.

I used to have a string of after-dinner tricks, some of which I picked up from Angus. I would jump back and forth over a held-up poker or cane, walk two or three steps on my hind legs, show my tongue on request, count ten and perform most of those boring obedience chores like "sit-stay", "lie", "heel" and "come". But when I reached ten I chucked it in. I still "jump" and "speak", but the rest is rubbish for a seasoned dog. For a time I tried to spice up the counting by licking my person's hand between each proffered paw, but that only prolonged the whole

thing and you'll find, Mopsy, that as you grow older, you lose patience.

Angus used to chase his tail round and round like a mad thing until dizzy, when he would stop and look at his audience with his slanting eyes and wait for the applause. He knew that none of them could compete with his performance. He would also dance with either of my people if exhilarated by rousing music, especially military marches. And, funnily enough, he always thought electricians and plumbers were in need of light relief. If he found them on all fours, lifting floor boards, he would pop a battered saliva-soaked football on their backs and suggest a game.

One hundred friendly sniffs, Suki

Dear Pup,

I am sorry for you. You do have a rotten time with fill-ins. Do you think Aunt Lynne is a miser?

The symptoms of this progressive and unhappy disease are:

1) A dustbin never more than half-full.
2) Frequent counting of money, checking change, arguing with barrow boys and reading flimsy sheets of paper called "balance sheets" or "bank statements".
3) Words like "thrift" and "bargain" in constant use; also "extravagance" and "dear" which may be accompanied by a disdainful sniff.
4) Plastic bags, brown paper, gift wrappings and string hoarded for further use. Frequent stopping in road to pick up rubber bands dropped by postman.
5) A cheap diet for you (i.e. pet mince from the least attractive butcher), which will be returned again and again to your plate until finished. Good quality tinned meat will only be served when it is found on special offer.
6) Much street walking in search of bargains.
7) Extreme reluctance to open purse or wallet.

If desperate, Mopsy, fake illness. Vets usually recommend a diet of chicken and veal for sick dogs. Eat the kind of grass which makes you vomit. Try rushing from the room whenever the hateful mince appears, as though it is about to cause you a mental breakdown. Bimbo, who has developed this ruse into a fine art to avoid his special diet when staying with friends, wins paws down every time.

But keep wagging. It's not for long. With luck your special person will be home soon with a bouncing baby and smiles all over her face.

Two licks for each ear and one for your nose,

Suki

Dear Pup,

When that boring old aunt lords it over you, just remember how ridiculous, and how inferior humans are in lots of ways.

Have you noticed, they can't even recognise the purr of their own cars or hear thunder until it is almost on top of them. And are you aware that they send pee away in bottles to be studied by white-coated technicians to discover information we can sniff out in moments? I believe that's a pretty costly affair, too. Oh dear, what a waste!

When my friend Shevy's person was told off for letting her stray on the part of the Green now reserved for humans, she replied. "Well, at least dogs don't have VD" which is obviously another stud in our collars, whatever it may mean, because it silenced the specist.

So keep wagging and don't be worn down by criticism, which is sometimes caused by envy.

Love, Suki

Dear Pup,

Please don't despair. I can't bear it. Once your people have started to take little Michael for granted, they'll love you more than you ever believed possible. Try to become INVOLVED with him.

My special person read aloud a piece from *The Times* newspaper the other day about a father and winner of the world's greatest prize for writing — the Noble or Nobel or something — who lost all inspiration when his adored dalmatian passed on to the land where every meal's a steak.

"Since Blemie died," he cried to his spouse, "everything has gone wrong. All this is the end of us . . . I won't be able to work any more — and when I can't work I shall die." Man and wife sat in the firelight and wept. So you see sensitive people often pine for their dogs as much as dogs pine for them. And Mopsy, every mother needs a calm and friendly PRESENCE to keep up her morale. I came to this home fearful of boys and men, but now I would not be without the man of the house and young Benedict, who rubs me up the right way, plays catch-me-if-you-can, and is generally useful when I need him. So stop wingeing, spruce up and put your nose back into joint.

All love and licks, Suki

Dear Pup,

Surely with your stocky little haunches you could beg very prettily and what about catching? My cousin Trixie is a phenomenal catcher and, as a result, saves a lot of washing-up, but I have butter jaws and therefore pretend it is beneath my dignity. But do choose the right moment, Mopsy; usually twenty minutes to or twenty past the hour is best, when often an unexpected pause in even the most excited human conversation occurs. My Scottish friend, Fergus, used to begin his performance too soon at dinner parties, before the guests were warmed by wine and now, in consequence, he's banished upstairs until the coffee stage when people are more prepared to hear his voice and see a pretend rat torn to shreds.

I must stop now because of a touch of cramp in my claws.

Lots of friendly sniffs and a benign lick in each ear,

Suki

Dear Pup,

Perhaps a pet of your own would lift the depression? Did I ever tell you that for years, to my terrier friends' fury, tame rodents revolutionised my life?

Picture me, Mopsy, eyes agog, tongue out, in front of a glass-fronted fish tank transformed by Benedict into a huge adventure playground for a lone mouse he found risking certain death from cats or cars in the Goldhawk Road. Nothing mattered to me except that little white figure trying out the rearranged obstacles. How quickly will she run down the newest toilet roll's tunnel? Can she still leap from branch to nest-top now that both have been moved? Will she hold that brown nut delicately as a Norwegian hooded rat does or gobble it noisily like a guinea pig? Rodents are so fascinating to study and such a joy to watch that, after Mouse left for a cheesier land, I had to shake myself ten times a day for a week to knock out the doldrums.

And, Mopsy, if you become as besotted as I was, your people will be wildly jealous and that's an excellent situation. They will leave Baby, to divert your attention. You will have TAUGHT them a LESSON.

Give it a thought and see if you can wangle anything. Guinea pigs, incidentally, also make charming pets for soft-hearted dogs.

Sorry – must close now. Delicious smells coming from kitchen, and I don't want to miss out. Keep wagging. Good luck.

Love and licks, Suki

Dear Pup,

Sorry you haven't heard from me lately. We've had a wedding here, because one of my people wants to be a wife and is going over the sea to live in Canada with her boyfriend. So there's been no end of a fuss the last few weeks with workers in and out building another room called a conservatory, and endless talk of clothes, photographs, food and hymns, with all sorts of names bandied about, which is terribly confusing for a dog who is trying to understand what is HAPPENING. One way and another, Mopsy, it's been a pretty unsettling time.

I can't actually see why we are celebrating, because we're going to lose Joanna — one-time owner of the furry slippers Angus tore up, and very useful to fall back on when my special person goes away on a project without me.

It was pretty hairy on the DAY, too. I was shut upstairs while everyone went to church — Joanna in an outsize car — to ask God to put in a word in favour of the event or something. Then they came back and, to be honest, Mopsy, my home was invaded by guests. There were literally DOZENS of them everywhere, buzzing away like wasps, and a table laden with food, and the whole place smelling of flowers and salmon.

I thought there was nothing in it for a dog, except a crushed paw or two, but Trixie, the only canine guest, latched on to Tato's special person who had noticed the humans weren't exactly wolfing down the sliced ham. Anna falls for a melting glance from any dog and so, I don't need to tell you, Trixie made it HER day.

There were guests in our house that night, even a couple in Joanna's bed, which disturbed me, because she, of course, had left with the young man, who, by the way, grew up with dogs so does at least know how to rub them up the RIGHT way. But, in my opinion the whole thing was a MISTAKE, because, to be honest, Joanna has been one of the family all the time I've been here and Angus helped to bring her up, so she could be TRUSTED and would actually share any good luck with any half-way decent dog. I was her pin-up too, but the huge picture of me above her bed flew away with her to Canada, along with a pile of presents. One way and another I don't think weddings have much to recommend them. A long day in Richmond Park rounded off with a good meal would surely be a better and healthier way of celebrating. Anyway I must rush now because I smell dinner on the hob, but I wanted you to know why I haven't written for so long.

Love, Suki

P.S. I hope the baby is not breaking any more nights.

Dear Pup,

I saw my famous acquaintance, the actor fellow Roly, on the Green today. He's rather harum-scarum, you know. I think all the concentration he needs on the set goes to his head a bit. He's very handsome and friendly, but he never stops long to

BBC TV

talk and is always looking over his shoulder to see who else is around. Of course, he's used to an audience and is recognised wherever he goes, which gives him a special air of confidence.

He's been visiting old people in Hammersmith Hospital and may tour the Children's Ward next, so he's bound to see himself as Royalty. I expect he's ranked higher than Princess Di or any of that lot. But it must be very odd to live half your time with the EastEnders and the rest here in Chiswick, where we are all pretty placid and I suppose every-day. Well there *is* Tato of course, who sees himself as a Chinese emperor, although he looks to me like one of those zip-up pyjama case dogs children keep on their pillows; AND little steel-grey Bimbo, who has a world-weary air and reminds the man in our house of some Frenchman called Verlaine. Bimbo has indeed lived in France and Dubai. He has flown in helicopters and planes and sailed across the sea, and survived six months in solitary as a punishment for leaving Britain. But NONE of us has appeared on the BOX, nor have we had our pictures in the newspapers as far as I know. Personally I hate being photographed, although I always try to stay still as it seems so desperately important to my people and is apparently quite a costly affair.

Tell me more about your dog friends next time you write, and DO keep your paw on the throb of canine life. People who won't let dogs speak to each other are an ABOMINATION. Supposing THEY were only allowed to talk to DOGS? Huh! What an outcry there would be. But I mustn't get hot under the collar about this, because if I start scratching my people will think I've caught fleas and I shall have to wear two* — such a bore and my basket clothes will be sprayed with horrible powder.

Licks and love,

Suki

*i.e., a special flea collar bought from the pet shop, as well as my own which Bimbo's people kindly brought me back from Cannes — wherever that may be.

Dear Pup,

I think some people are becoming more canine.
When I was at Trixie's place some weeks ago,
helping care for the house while her people were in
Canada, I found a new spirit, contrary to recent
apartheid developments in London. Things, by the
way, can be a bit dicey at the Old Parsonage, because
sometimes Trixie carries her German Schnautzer
property protection image a bit far (e.g., she enjoys
riding in my car but won't let me in hers). But this
time she was quite mellow and we enjoyed several
trips together and gossiped about our special people
who, being twins, came from the same litter and are
therefore pretty well alike.

Anyway to get to the point, Mopsy, on one of our
outings we were actually INVITED INTO a church, by

an official-looking lady who found us waiting politely in the porch.

"We like dogs to have a look round," she said.

So, quiet as huskies, and expecting to see God, we went inside on leads, much awed by the strange scent that hung on the air like a blue mist and the general feeling of no-fun-and-games. Of course, I was terrified that Trixie might leave a message on one of those kneeler things to mark the occasion, but no, she walked beside me, very soberly, disappointed that there was no grass and not a rabbit or canine post office within sniff, and quite unimpressed by statues and stained glass windows. But, although our tails stayed down, and we were glad to be outside again, we did try to show some appreciation, and, on reflection, felt that another discriminatory barrier had fallen – although naturally sad that God, whose name our people call so often, wasn't at home. Anyway, Mopsy, I should be grateful if you would report the incident to Fetch, as I gather he's still active on the Dog Liberation Front.

To change the topic, I went to Chiswick House today and met by chance one of those foreign dogs who are too small for their skins. She hadn't much to say for herself, which isn't surprising because she has the head of a HIPPO and I understand those animals are too large for their brains. I can't understand why so many people are buying alien dogs when there are so many well-made English ones crying out for homes. I mean a bull mastiff could blow spots off a rottweiler any day and as for dobermanns, well they simply haven't adjusted to the British way of life and are a total failure on the Green.

Must stop now because I have a crick in my neck.

Love and licks, Suki

P.S. Yes, of course it's impossible to become involved with a baby who never raises his head from the pillow, however sweet you are. I didn't realise human puppies were so grossly retarded. Do you mean to say he's simply going to lie there for six months and won't be house-trained for a YEAR? That's incredible! No wonder more and more women are opting for dogs instead. And aren't we supposed to be the DUMB ones! But cheer up, if he turns out like Benedict with a generous heart and a penchant for chips and kebabs, the waiting will have been worthwhile.

More licks from an ever-loving, Suki

Dear Pup,

The trouble about shopping at Christmas-time or waiting for trains is that there are so many LEGS. It is horrible to be below the KNEES, much worse than running through the deepest undergrowth. And where there are suitcases as well – ouch – there's no room for any dog smaller than an alsatian. I slipped my collar on Reading platform once in my confusion. Listen carefully and if SHOPPING comes into the conversation, refuse to leave home. I always watch my person dressing, if she puts on elegant clothes I know the day is not for me, and retire to bed with a resigned sigh.

There was a fight on the Green yesterday but I wasn't involved because being a pacifist, I don't fight by choice unless there's a fence between me and the other dog(s).

I don't think you should pick quarrels. Feuds are so boring and being sewn up is quite a costly affair. Why spoil a good walk for youself and others? And do remember, you are rather a SMALL dog with easy-to-shred ears and a somewhat impractical mouth. An alsatian or bull terrier could tear you to tatters and then your special person might suffer a heart attack. And that would be a very unnecessary and sad end for you both. So DO control yourself and try to be the jolly friendly little dog your name conjures up.

Licks and love from a perturbed Suki

Dear Pup,

Do tell Tilly not to worry about spending Christmas alone with her person. The days are sure to pass in a not unpleasant haze of nostalgia, and no doubt she will have half the chicken, instead of just the giblets which might otherwise have been her lot. Likewise chocolates, biscuits and other goodies. She can also bask in the satisfaction of knowing she has saved an abandoned human from slipping away into DEPRESSION.

As you know relations often don't make proper provisions for a dog and might well have objected to Tilly finding herself a comfortable armchair or wanting a slice of turkey. I've heard of hostesses actually tying canine guests to table legs. Can you imagine it? Angus, of course, always chewed through his lead in such circumstances, but I would shrink into a ridiculous little heap of discarded doggy flesh and bones.

In haste – licks, Suki

Dear Pup,

A terrible thing happened yesterday. My people gave a buffet supper for seventeen friends: soup, turkey and bacon pilaff, fruit and cheese, quite a simple affair which nevertheless filled the kitchen all day with the most mouth-watering smells.

Of course I looked forward to my share, especially when my special person tied a red ribbon round my neck and told me I was an honoured guest. So although the only dog invited, I put on my best party expression and welcomed everyone with all the quiet charm I could muster, and then moved freely among them, licking a hand here and there, and lots of the visitors remarked on my delightful manners and general sophistication. But when the food was served I was — would you believe it — subjected to the most blatant canine discrimination. To put it sharply, Mopsy, EVERYONE was fed but ME. Although astonished, I tried to remain very calm, pacing back and forth as plates were carried to the hungry guests, but when it came to second helpings, I knew I had been overlooked on purpose and there was now little time to lose, which was all the more hurtful because my people have always claimed to hate — not dislike, mark you, but hate — apartheid or racism of any kind.

"Suki," I said to myself, you may be small, but you have an important place in the life of this family and you've kept your special person company in the hot kitchen all day, and now is the time to put your paw down." In short, I had to think quickly of a demo, which would shame my humans without losing my own reputation for charm and sophistication. My chance came when I saw Bruin and Bimbo's person put her plate on a low coffee table. There was no meat left on it, but a few grains of rice and chopped vegetables, which I usually refuse.

Bimbo.

All eyes, were on me, Mopsy, as I walked across that room and, with dignified aplomb, ate every morsel. The fact that I NEVER normally steal from tables drove the message home like the thrust of a knife. The sudden silence told me that everyone knew I was MAKING A POINT. And my special person rushed with cries of remorse to serve me a liberal helping of the fast disappearing pilaff, which, although I was starving, I ate with the utmost delicacy, savouring the garlic and herbs with obvious relish.

I don't want to blow my own hunting horn, but I think my behaviour was an example of how a thinking dog can, with quiet dignity and great firmness, change human attitudes and I believe that evening I made local canine history. Anyway I must stop now because pride comes before a tumble and I don't want any more visits to the vet. Write soon.

Love and licks, Suki

Dear Mopsy,

I'm sorry I slipped back into calling you Pup. Yes, of course you're grown-up now, but to me you'll always be young, new and struggling in a world of confused and confusing humanity.

And Mopsy do STOP worrying about lack of papers. As I've said a hundred times: IT DOESN'T MATTER. I have three servants (my people), a delightful house and all the cherishing I want, simply on the strength of a receipt saying four pounds fifty pence, received with thanks, like those scraps people are given when they pay the newspaper bill. It is headed with the name of the Dogs' Home, but doesn't describe my age, colour or sex. My special human nevertheless keeps it most carefully and never tires of telling friends how lucky she was to pick me out in a run full of oddments. Of course, to be fair, most of the others were dying of distemper, so there wasn't much competition. Did I tell you I nearly died, too? Well I mustn't rattle on, because I expect you're busy checking the baby's presents. I only want to knock that rock off your shoulder. Stick your nose in the air, when people talk about pedigrees, and walk like a princess. It's style that matters, not who your forebears were.

Keep wagging and make sure you have a gift this year.

Love, Suki

P.S. I enclose copy of receipt for you to see.

Dear Mopsy,

Have I ever mentioned to you an attractive female dog called Sam? She's black and tan, like me only larger and short-coated and, I think, now seventeenish. I used to meet her in the street quite often when we lived in the other house which was near hers. But my friendly overtures were always rejected. I suspect, Mopsy, that Sam left her brothers and sisters before she learned to play or, perhaps, she was an ONLY. Anyway she's pretty well fixated on her special person who, to cut a long story short, used to talk to my person a lot and is one of those publishers who buy from humans like mine all those pages they write morning, noon and night and turn them into books, which is, I think, quite a feat.

But, to return to the point, this publisher and her firm want to take my letters to you, print and bind them and sell them to bookshops. What do you think?

I was a bit sniffy at first — well I'm not sure I want my private thoughts passed from hand to hand, but then my special person said if I agreed to the contract I could have chicken breasts three times a week and paté on Saturdays, and a slice of smoked salmon every so often. She also promised a Scottish holiday next year on the proceeds. Well, Mopsy, I wandered about the house with a bit of a watery mouth, seeing the turn the conversation had taken. Then suddenly, quick as lightning, my mind was made up. I shook myself, wagged my tail, and looked

Sam.

my person straight in the face, eyeball to eyeball, which is my way of saying "All right. Go ahead. Terms accepted."

Apparently these letters belong to me, not you, but I thought I should give you a chance to bark your head off if you don't like the idea — there is that one about you and Fetch after all. But, now that I have that new menu within sniffing distance, NOTHING will change my mind. So there it is. We're going to be famous which puts that pedigree business into perspective once and for all.

Write soon. Love and licks from your budding author friend, Suki

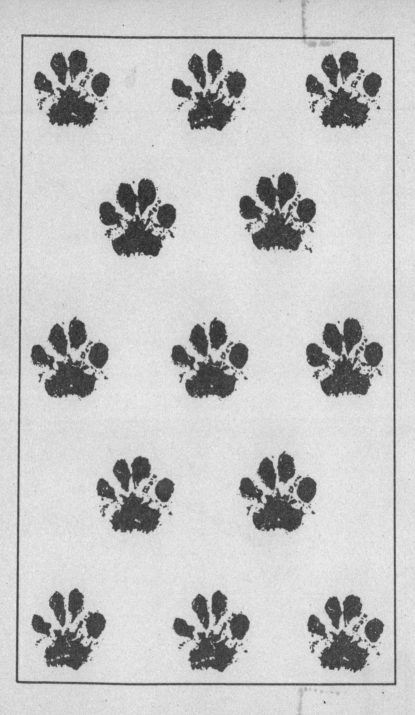